I0158790

Wise (and not so wise) advice from the Great Philosophers

Family values, sex and a little bit of philosophy

Do we need to go into this? But we do. Because there are plenty of philosophers offering advice on intimate human relationships where wiser souls might instead have stuck to discussing their 'hypotheticals'. From Aristotle insisting on men treating woman as domestic cattle, to Diogenes. ah, 'relieving' himself in public, no matter what your personal liking is, a philosopher can be found trying to make it sound reasonable.

For better or (more likely) for worse, here are some of philosophy's most celebrated ideas and arguments on love.

Martin Cohen has established a worldwide reputation as a radical philosopher and unconventional thinker. His two introductions to philosophy, *101 Philosophy Problems* and *101 Ethical Dilemmas* have been translated into many different languages including an underground, *samizdat* version in Iran. He has also written an 'anti-history' of great philosophers, called *Philosophical Tales* and is the author of the UK edition of *Philosophy for Dummies*.

'How to Love'

Wise (and not so wise) advice from
the Great Philosophers

By Martin Cohen

The Media Studies Unit
Lewes

First published 2014 by The Media Studies Unit,
No. 23, South Street, Lewes, United Kingdom

Copyright © 2014 Martin Cohen

Typeset in Gill Sans Light by the Media Studies Unit

ISBN: 978-0-9576927-7-0 (Paper)
ISBN: 978-0-9576927-8-7 (ebook)

British Library Cataloguing in Publication Data
A British Library catalogue record has been requested.

BIC Subject Categories: HPX Popular philosophy

BISAC Category: Philosophy/General

To Judit, a philosopher of every day life

The mind seeks its own good, even though, like a drunkard, it often cannot find the path home.

Boethius

(*The Consolation of Philosophy,* Book III, part ii)

Contents

'How to Live'

Wise (and not so wise) advice from
the Philosophers on Everyday Life

Introduction to the series of mini-books

How to eat well, get laid and make lots of money. It's
philosophy, Jim—but not as we know it.

Yet even if you've been brought up to believe that philosophy
is remorseless logic and lots of sensible ethics with only
occasionally a little bit of metaphysics for light relief, the secret
of philosophy is that it has always *really* been a very practical
guide to everyday life. In fact, from Pythagoras to Poincaré,
from Socrates to Schopenhauer, philosophers have always
been the go-to experts on *everything*. That's why, even now,
two thousand odd years after their views were first set out,
the great philosophers are still inspiring, if not exactly
informing, management gurus, TV programme makers and
marketing experts too. It's a longevity that has something to
do both with the timelessness of our concerns—and the
excellence of their advice.

Don't be confused by the fact that these days philosophy is
presented as something rather dry and technical, to do with
ontologies and essences, categorical imperatives and
suppressed premises, because that is only a very recent
version. Instead, keep away from the professors in the big
universities, who write long books full of footnotes. Because,

in fact, philosophy is, and has always been a very different kind of activity: a hands-on affair offering advice about practical matters and life's most pressing concerns.

From where to buy a holiday house, to what time to get out of bed, to how to chat up someone, a philosopher has been there and thought out the smart policy for us already. Alas, at some point, the idea of turning to the local philosopher in order to become wise (an entirely natural assumption) was lost. Instead along came scientists and specialists of all sorts offering philosophy-free solutions to the problems of the world.

So complete was the philosophical fall from public grace that by the early 20th century, Bertrand Russell's book, *The Conquest of Happiness* (1930), written at a really rather depressing point in history, was only prepared to offer mealy-mouthed platitudes, or as he put it, to:

> ...suggest a cure for the ordinary day-to-day unhappiness from which most people in civilised countries suffer, and which is all the more unbearable because, having no obvious external cause, appears inescapable.

In the modern world, it seemed, the only role left for philosopher gurus was to endlessly recycle earnest advice to have faith, work hard and never to despair.

The truth is very different. Behind the spurious technicism of the scientific experts of today, and beyond the equally spurious generalities of the self-help guides, is a surprisingly detailed and insightful body of philosophical wisdom. Yet maybe we should not be too surprised as after all, philosophers have had a long time to work on it. As long ago as five thousand years ago (2700 BCE), they were pushing advice that sounds almost like the stuff we read today on internet blogs. Ancient texts reveal that when the Yellow Emperor, of Ancient China, asked his Chief Minister, Qi Bo, why it was that 'people nowadays' did not live as long, Qi Bo replied that it was because in the past people practiced the Tao, and appreciated the flow of yin and yang and the principle of balance in all things. But 'these days', he warned:

> People have changed their way of life. They drink wine as though it were water, indulge in destructive activities, drain their *jing* and deplete their *qi*... Seeking emotional excitement and monetary pleasures, people disregard the natural rhythm and order of the universe. They fail to regulate their lifestyle and diet, and sleep improperly.

Sound familiar? But nothing is new under the sun. That's why turning to long-dead philosophers from bygone eras can be a surprisingly productive life strategy for the world of today.

---

* In traditional Chinese medicine, *jing*, is the body's essence and *qi*, is the life energy.

MAKE LOVE LIKE A PHILOSOPHER

Family Values, Sex and a little bit of philosophy

Do we need to go into this? But we do. Because there are plenty of philosophers offering advice on intimate human relationships where wiser souls might instead have stuck to discussing their hypotheticals. From Aristotle insisting on men treating woman as domestic cattle, to Diogenes 'relieving' himself in public, no matter what is your personal proclivity, a philosopher can be found trying to make it sound reasonable. For better or (more likely) for worse, here are some of philosophy's most dodgy arguments.

Actually, many of the great philosophers stayed unmarried, such as Descartes, Spinoza, Leibniz, and Kant. Plato too is thought not have remained single, but the exception to the rule is Socrates, who married the young Xanthippe (the marriage produced a little boy), although he only tied the knot when he was in his sixties. But enough of that— what about sex?

Diotima, the lady philosopher who inspired Plato and Socrates, suggested that sex and indeed lust (particularly for those much younger than yourself) was part of a very virtuous quest, inspired by the desire for beauty and immortality. Rushing to the opposite extreme, Saint Augustine roundly condemned pleasure in general and sex in particular, concluding that human biology was part of what he called the 'Original Sin'.

Although Plato recalls Diotima's argument apparently appreciatively, he spends much more time in his books describing the advantages of the rational organisation of reproduction, in an early and wholly discreditable attempt to create a master race. The tone of philosophy was then set by Hegel, who put conflict and fear at the heart of the dialectical marriage, while Hegel's arch-enemy, Schopenhauer, contributed the insight that sex was the paramount feature of human existence—'the fundamental urge'. Forget the 'selfish gene', the idea that sex is the key to everything has been around a long time.

Remain faithful to Kant

The first thing to do if you fall in love is see a lawyer

Immanuel Kant, often counted as the central figure in *modern* philosophy, had strong views on the passionate demands of love. In one of his lectures to students he says:

> In loving from sexual inclination, we make the person into an object of their appetite. As soon as the person is possessed, and the appetite sated, they are thrown away, *as one throws away a lemon after sucking the juice from it.* The sexual impulse can, admittedly, be combined with human affection, and then it also carries with it the aims of the latter, but if it is taken in and by itself, it is nothing more than appetite. So considered, there lies in this inclination a degradation of man; for as soon as anyone becomes an object of another's appetite, all motives of moral relationship fall away; as object of the other's appetite, that person is in fact a thing, whereby the other's appetite is sated, and can be misused as such a thing by anybody.

What was Kant thinking of? Sadomasochism? Saucy wood-engravings? Thomas de Quincey, who knew him better than anyone, wrote in *Blackwood's Magazine* in the early nineteenth century, that Kant's personal life was much more interesting than his philosophy, a view which Graham Bird of Manchester University says 'would now be regarded as odd to the point of perversity'. Professor Bird thinks instead that Kant's 'transcendental apperception' and 'noumena' are much more interesting, and indeed, he points out, since they led to 'anomalous monism', they must also be considered the much more *important*.

However, in matters of the heart, we can afford to be a little perverse. For Kant's eternal contribution to philosophy is a set of rules. And rules are also what defined his personal life. First off, premarital sex and any sexual act that was not a means of procreation is immoral. In his *Metaphysics*, he even calls it 'cannibalistic', saying 'carnal enjoyment is cannibalistic in principle… each is actually a consumable thing to the other'.

Worse than that, premarital sex is also *foolish* as one's sexual attributes should not be given away without a proper contract. Marriage provides that, affording both sides 'lifelong possession of each other's sexual attributes' as he puts it rather unromantically*.

Some people might be put off not just being foolish but even of getting married by this talk. But Kant allows that 'natural' sex, meaning the variety by which 'procreation of some kind' is possible, contractually arranged by marriage, is less awful than 'unnatural' use of the sexual organs. This sort of thing, he explains, 'takes place either with a person of the same sex or with an animal of a nonhuman species'.

As for what Kant calls 'unnatural vice', (I'll let the reader speculate as to what that is for themselves) this is really the worst. The 'unnatural use (and so misuse) of one's sexual attribute is a violation of one's duty to oneself', he says. Indeed, since Kant says these sorts of things are 'contrary to morality in the highest degree', we might assume there is a 'Categorical Imperative' against it. But curiously, Kant's famous ethical rule seems to fall short of what is required here by puritans, since it implores us only to;

'Act only according to a maxim by which you can at the same time wish that it shall become a general law'

–and unnatural vice is nothing if not universalisable

But then indeed, Kant's own policy of strict celibacy doesn't seem to be truly universalisable, as then the human race would die out. Not that is necessarily a problem for the theory, as Kant always argued that moral principles are to be followed unconditionally and without regard for the consequences. That is what makes his 'imperative' so categorical. For example, why it is always necessary to tell the truth, even to that madman hunting his victim (or to your partner the day after cheating on them). And equally, why this is supposed to explain why someone who never does anything to hurt anyone else is actually not a good person if their actions are prompted merely by fear of going to prison, or why a tradesperson who is always helpful and honest is not being virtuous if underneath they simply intend by so doing to improve their sales. In a way, this is 'ancient' ethics. By comparison, Adam Smith, writing at the same time, was offering something new by cheerfully constructing his moral system around 'enlightened self-interest' operating within a social setting. But Smith was known by his friends for little ethical foibles, such as helping himself to extra sugar when at his Gentleman's Club in Edinburgh—just for the pleasure! Imagine the logical problems if everyone did that.

It is easy to think from Kant's strictures against sex that he was a harsh man, but nothing could be further from the truth. With regard to the 'fair sex' he was nothing if not respectful— even a tiny bit romantic. Thomas de Quincey relates how towards the end of his life, Kant fell in the street and was helped up by two young women. Some time later, when he had recovered himself, Kant thanked them profusely… and gave them a red rose.

The commonsense fact is, couples, and families, let alone societies, need to allow a little space for self-interest, alongside the rules. But then Kant never married, although he did have some discussion of romantic matters with correspondents such as one admirer called Maria von Herbert. (A story I also relate in my book *Philosophical Tales*).

Maria wrote to Kant, in 1791, to say that she had long been a fan of his, and had recently applied Kant's 'truth-telling principle' in her most intimate affections. Alas, it seems that by telling her lover of 'a previous affair', she caused him to be offended. Although 'there was no vice in it', she explains, 'the lie was enough, and his love has vanished'. As an honorable man, 'her lover offered to continue as... 'a friend'. Oh dear! That bad! Maria confides to Kant that the inner feeling 'that once, unbidden, led us to each other' is no more—'and my heart splinters into a thousand burning pieces!'

So far so tragic. Maria adds that it was only Kant's strictures against committing suicide that had thus far stopped her from taking that way out. Kant wrote back promptly the following spring (this is before email slowed down the rate of correspondence). After a few kindly words on her evident good intentions, he speaks sternly to remind her of her duty. He warns that lies cause contracts to be voided and to lose their force, and that this is a wrong done to mankind generally. 'To be truthful in all declarations, therefore, is a sacred and absolutely commanding decree of reason, limited by no expediency.'

If such full frankness leads a couple to split asunder, this is because their 'affection is more physical than moral' and would soon have disappeared anyway. This, sighs Kant, the confirmed bachelor, is a misfortune often to be encountered in life. Fortunately, the value of life itself, when it depends on the enjoyment we get from people, 'is vastly over-rated'.

Maria replied a year later, to say that she had now achieved the high level of moral exactitude outlined by Kant, albeit that she now found her time rather empty. Instead, she says, she feels indifferent to everything, and suffers from ill health. Like the best moral philosophers, 'Each day interests me only to the extent that it brings me closer to death.' She thinks she would like to visit Kant, however, as in his portrait she has discerned 'a profound calm there, and moral depth—if not the acuity of which the *Critique of Pure Reason* is proof'. She entreats 'her God' to 'give me something that will get this intolerable emptiness out of my soul'.

But for that, apparently, Kant had nothing to offer.

2

Lust like Schopenhauer

It's only natural

Schopenhauer and Kant had a lot in common, and yet in other ways were polar opposites. They lived in the same historical period (Schopenhauer would have been 16 when Kant died), both wrote in German, and both remained bachelors all their lives. Yet if Kant seems to have lived an almost monastic existence, and was highly admired by everyone, Schopenhauer comes across as a much more worldly, even oafish figure, and his work has often been dismissed for that reason too.

But it is on the subject of human sexuality where the difference between the two thinkers is most plain. Where Kant sees sex as a necessary evil (that he himself avoids) and prefers to speculate on the world beyond sense perception, Schopenhauer says refreshingly:

> The genitals are the life-preserving principle
> assuring to time endless life. In this capacity
> they were worshipped by the Greeks as the
> phallus and by the Hindus as the lingam, which
> are therefore the symbol of the affirmation of
> the will.

Or *Der Wille*, in German. (Now you know where the English slang term for the male appendage comes from.) Where Kant and indeed the whole of Western society frowned upon casual sex and venerated the institution of marriage,

Schopenhauer takes the opposite line, frowning on marriage and defending all sorts of extra-marital sex as merely natural. In his Journal, Schopenhauer describes the moment of 'ecstasy in the act of copulation' as the only time when we really know the 'true essence and core of all things, the goal and the purpose of all existence'. This is the Eastern vision that can also be seen reflected in the advice of Diotima to Socrates, recorded by Plato. (Schopenhauer is rare among Western philosophers for actually studying Eastern texts.)

And it seems that Schopenhauer pursued his research into 'the purpose of all existence' in a practical sense too. Alas, there is no evidence that Schopenhauer ever managed to treat any women with respect. His sister, Adele, who he eventually fell out with over money, complained about his reporting in a letter 'two love affairs without love' adding: 'May you not totally lose the ability to esteem a woman while dealing with the common and base ones of our sex and may Heaven one day lead you to a woman to whom you can feel something deeper than these infatuations.'

Only in 1821, now aged thirty three, did he fall in love with an opera singer, called Caroline Richter. She was just 19 when they met in Berlin. However, it seems that the fragrant Caroline often carried on affairs with several men simultaneously, and Schopenhauer greatly resented the fact that ten months into a trip he made to Italy, she has a baby. The father was a theatre employee called Louis Medon—*not even a philosopher.*

When Schopenhauer moved from Berlin to Frankfurt, he offered to take Caroline with him—but refused to allow her to bring her son. Caroline would not abandon her child, and so, after a short correspondence. their relationship ended for good. Given both his reputation and indeed his cynical philosophy of life, it is perhaps surprising to find that Schopenhauer, almost thirty years later, at the age of seventy—one, added a codicil to his will leaving Caroline five thousand talers*. (Although even this thought was soured by a provision that the money should not benefit 'Carl Ludwig Gustav Medon', as the child was called).

But back to the time of the break-up, and soon after, now at the age of 43, Schopenhauer's roving eye fell on, Flora Weiss a rather tasty-looking 17-year-old girl at a boat party in Germany. Not one to waste time, he immediately approached Flora with a bunch of grapes as a suitable offering, and announced both his attraction and his intention of speaking to her father about marriage. This indeed he did, although Flora`s father was taken aback at first and responded, 'But she is a mere child!' Later, however, in deference to philosophy, he agreed to let Flora decide. Which she did, and her answer was a firm 'no'. Decades later, she described the effect of Arthur's gift of the grapes saying 'But I didn't want them, you see. I felt revolted because old Schopenhauer had touched them. And so I let them slide, quite gently, into the water behind me.'

Did Flora not know of the ancient link between grapes and fertility?

Pillow talk

Poor old Schopenhauer! It shouldn't happen to a great philosopher. But then, as he says 'der Wille' is irrational. Add to which, his philosophy shows that life is meaningless. Birth leads to death and the only purpose of activity between the two seems to be to produce offspring who can then repeat the cycle. There is nothing behind the life-force (der Wille)— no strategy, no reason, no purpose. It is primary, outside space and time, it sweeps perception before it, it determines our concepts, it dictates all actions. It even drives evolution, not the other way around as Darwin would have it. Schopenhauer explains:

> That human life must be a kind of mistake is sufficiently clear from the fact that man is a compound of needs, which are difficult to satisfy; moreover, if they are satisfied, all he is granted is a state of painlessness, in which he can only give himself up to boredom. This is a precise proof that existence in itself has no value.

On the Emptiness of Existence

Similarly, in another essay called the 'Metaphysics of Love', Schopenhauer says, with 24 carat bitterness: 'We see a pair of lovers exchanging longing glances—yet why so secretly, timidly and stealthily? Because these lovers are traitors secretly striving to perpetuate all the misery and turmoil that otherwise would come to a timely end.

Alas, just as the life-force is totally irrational, so too the will to live and the will to procreate obey no rules and accept no logic. Schopenhauer's grisly tale of the Australian ant, nasty example of its kind, demonstrates this. When decapitated, it turns into two grotesque fighting machines—both determined to sting the other to death. Just like a divorcing couple...

But it is his book, *The World as Will and Representation*, that is the true end product of his insight, written in a non-academic style, with an ironic, aristocratic tone. Indeed, in later life, Schopenhauer tried to live as an aristocrat too, adopting a self-consciously leisurely existence as a 'great thinker'. Like Kant, whom he praises, he dressed in an old-fashioned way, ate at strictly regular times, and took a daily walk, in his case, in the company of his much-loved poodle, Atma. Apart from occasional visits to the theatre and reading the newspapers at the public library, he was the model of a scholarly recluse. As he had put it, when originally challenged as to why he was abandoning the business career his parents had planned for him: 'Life is a difficult question; I have decided to spend my life in thinking about it.'

Unlike Kant though, for a long time, though, no one was interested in Schopenhauer's ideas, let alone in his philosophy of existence. Despite having a celebrity mother, he had trouble even getting anyone to print a few hundred copies of his book.

After a series of delays in obtaining first publication, Schopenhauer wrote one of his characteristically abusive letters to the publisher, who replied coolly 'that he must decline all further correspondence with one whose letters, in their divine coarseness and rusticity, savoured more of the cabman than of the philosopher', before finishing by committing himself to print only with the hope that his fears that the work would be good for nothing but waste paper might not be realized…

It was only the second edition of *The World as Will and Representation* (in 1844) that was received with any appreciation. And now, where hitherto Schopenhauer had been known in Frankfurt mainly as the son of *the* Johanna Schopenhauer, now he came to have his own enthusiastic following. Artists painted his portrait; a bust of him was made by

Elizabeth Ney. One of his most enthusiastic German admirers was the A-list celebrity, Richard Wagner, who sent him a copy of his opera *The Ring of Nibelungen,* with the inscription: 'In admiration and gratitude.'

In a characteristically bitter yet pompous preface to the second edition, Schopenhauer dedicated the book 'Not to my contemporaries, not to my compatriots—to mankind I commit my now completed work, in the confidence that it will not be without value for them, even if this should be late recognized, as is commonly the lot of what is good.' Many authors think their books are too good for their readers, but unusually Schopenhauer seems to have been vindicated.

Certainly, when years later, Friedrich Nietzsche found a copy of *Die Welt als Wille und Vorstellung* in a second-hand bookstore he was unable to put the book down until he had finished it. And in London, Sigmund Freud would study Schopenhauer's description of the primal 'will to live' and 'sexual impulse' nothing less than avidly, before drawing up his own account of the *id* or 'life-instinct' and making the *libido* the central feature in human life. Yet it is not the Austrian psychoanalyst who wrote '…consciousness is the mere surface of our mind, of which, as of the earth, we do not know the inside, but only the crust', but this, still today, relatively obscure, German philosopher.

Schopenhauer always saw himself as a kind of metaphysical cryptographer who had stumbled on to the key to understanding the universe—which was this: sex. All the other grand theories are heading the wrong way. The urge to reproduce, the life force, instinct, 'desire', call it what you, er, will, is the ultimate underlying reality, the essential force. We are all so many puppets twitching and dancing to its whim, so many mayflies, created one day, dead the next, leaving only our eggs. Worse! Nature has more use for species than for individuals, and yet species too must come and go as part of the larger cycle. At the end of the day, we all seem to be rather insignificant.

There's a lesson in there somewhere.

---

* Schopenhauer was not rich but lived mainly off his inheritance which allowed him to spend about 1000 talers a year.

3

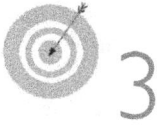

Respect family Unvalues

There are only grown-ups in Philosophy Heaven

'How, then, shall a man maintain the existence of society?' asked the Ancient Greek Stoic philosopher, Epictetus.

This is a fine lofty, question. Politicians address it all the time, tweaking taxes here, changing public policy there. Yet so can the rest of us, in referring to that smallest unit of society, the family. Epictetus, an unusual philosopher in being formerly a slave, speaks for many philosophers in recommending abstinence from sex, not having children, and certainly not having any extra-martial affairs.

The most important family value, for him, was to have no family.

> In the name of God, are those men greater benefactors to society who introduce into the world to occupy their own places two or three ugly-snouted, grunting children, or those who watch over, as far as they can all mankind, observing what they do, how they pass their days, what they care about, what they neglect contrary to their duty?
>
> *The Discourses*, by Epictetus

Pillow talk

There was a strong current in Ancient Greek thinking against families. That is why in Plato's Republic they are abolished. Like many would-be social progressives today, the Ancients though that families were 'unnatural', and hence to be done away with. Yet it does not require a deep philosophical insight to see that children do need bringing up, they cannot be left like so many frog-spawn in the pond. To this practical point, many philosophers (notably the Cynics) have variously said that it would be no harm if the human race were to die out (a consistent but unpersuasive line) or that childcare should be minimised, essentially by making it into something very like Plato's system in the Republic. All the children are collectively reared by everyone 'in a gaggle'.

Philosophers have not been particularly successful in terms of conventional family relationships. If Socrates seems to have got on passably well with his wife, Xanthippe (forty years his junior, mind you...) the mature Aristotle's attitude towards his 18 year old wife is indicated in his philosophising: he says women are a kind of domestic cattle that live in the house. As Andrew Schaffer says in his witty and insightful little book, *Great Philosophers who Failed in Love*, although we admire their wisdom in many things, it certainly does not extend to their conduct of family life.

Jean Jacques Rousseau personally, if regretfully, took all five of his children to a hospital for unwanted children, and G.W. H. Hegel, stern headteacher though he was, added an illegitimate child with his landlord's wife to his own flock of young Hegelians. Kant, Spinoza and Descartes were all bachelors, although Descartes had a daughter with a young woman who worked in the bookshop underneath his flat in Amsterdam. Actually, and perhaps surprisingly in view of his other attitudes, he seems to have been very fond of both of them and to have planned to look after both his lover and their child in a quiet corner of Holland using the 'cover story' that Helena was Descartes' servant and Francine was his niece. Alas, the young child died of Scarlet Fever and four years later the records show Helena married a local innkeeper.

Curious and touching note of history, is that Descartes himself provided the 1000-guilder dowry for Helena's wedding and stayed in the area for a number of years pursuing his researches, including his life-long passion for automata. But then Descartes was summoned by 'society' in the shape of the Queen of Sweden to teach philosophy. The Queen famously liked her lessons at the crack of dawn, a preference that caused the philosopher to catch cold and die of pneumonia there on 11 February 1650.

Thus fulfilling his duty to society, in travelling to Sweden to teach the Queen, cost Descartes to lose both his own life and that of his precious daughter, Francine (see box), for a second time.

The answer to Epictetus' question then is simple. Society can best be served by getting up early and freezing to death.

Descartes and Francine

The story goes that Descartes told the crew of the boat that was to take him to Sweden to teach the Queen that he would be travelling with his young daughter (despite this being some years after her death) and that he did not wish to be disturbed under any circumstances.

During the voyage, however, the boat was caught in a particularly dreadful storm and, fearing they would have to abandon ship, the crew burst into his quarters to wake him. What they found though there was not Descartes snoozing, let alone Francine, but only a large, sinister looking black trunk. The sailors, already consumed by curiosity by their mysterious passenger and his voyage, stole a look inside.

On opening the case they were astonished to find an incredibly lifelike, full sized doll of a lovely young girl - Francine. Touching it, their astonishment turned to terror when the doll sat upright and turned its eyes to look at them!

They rushed at once to show the delicately crafted automaton to the captain who, having never seen anything like it before, suspected it might be a work of black magic and possibly even the cause of the storm that was threatening to sink the boat. So he ordered the crew to throw it overboard into the cold, grey waters of the North Sea, where it was never seen again.

4

Move on to the higher forms of love

Of laws, institutes and buildings

There are two quite different descriptions of love and family life in Plato's writings. The most well known is rather grim: it consists of the male and female Philosopher-Guardians living in common, eating in communal messes and sleeping in dormitories. What is more, only the 'best specimens amongst them' will be allowed to produce the future rulers, to be brought up without useless emotional bonds, and without access to frivolities like music and books, but rather on a controlled diet of the Ancient Greek equivalent of rugby and raw beef. But part of this ascetic picture (which reflected the admired reality of the military regime in Ancient Sparta) is the assertion that 'true love' is better kept entirely 'theoretical'—more like the love between two members of the same family—a father and a son perhaps. Yet, since Plato's political vision starts by abolishing family relations, this kind of love seems to be abolished too.

That's one problem. There are others too, as Socrates admits to his friend, Glaucon.

> Possibly, if these proposals were carried out, they might be ridiculed as involving a good many breaches of custom.
>
> Indeed, Socrates, they might.

> The most ridiculous being the notion of
> women exercising naked along with the men
> in the wrestling schools; some of them elderly
> women too, like the old men who still have a
> passion for exercise when they are wrinkled
> and not very agreeable to look at...

So Plato is well aware of the practical limitations of his political recipe. Perhaps Plato's point about 'rational sex' also needs to be understood in the historical context of the Greek elite, where sex was conventionally a non-consensual affair between an older man and a young boy. Not here the homosexual love of contemporary culture.

'Platonic love', then, is a concept uprooted from its historical context, but more than that, does not reflect Plato's more considered view, which is set out in another dialogue called the *Symposium* (*Drinking Party*) playlet. It is here that we find Socrates in an unusually jocular mood, recalling how the wise woman, Diotima, had once told him that love was a step on the way to the understanding and appreciation of beauty and goodness. Indeed, not only that, but of the *ideal* forms of beauty and goodness. Diotima's lesson to Socrates was that the attraction to beauty, specifically attraction to beautiful naked bodies, is fundamental, but is best understood as being only a preliminary stage to something else. Looked at in this way love provides the foundation for Plato's Theory of Forms.

> You should use the things of this world as
> rungs on a ladder. You start by loving one
> attractive body and step up to two; from there
> to the beauty of people's activities, from there
> to the beauty of intellectual endeavours and
> from there you ascend to that final intellectual
> endeavour which is no more and no less than
> the study of that beauty, so that you finally
> recognise true beauty.

Or so Diotima advises Socrates. She adds that there is a natural link between seeing a beautiful body and wanting to have sex with it: behind the physical prompting is the more philosophical, if subconscious desire to 'make the beauty last forever'. In this way, sexual attraction and beauty are irrevocably linked.

If most of Plato's dialogues feature Socrates winning arguments, in this case he is a willing convert. In the *Symposium*, Socrates too praises personal love in a way that makes a surprising contrast to his normally stern words. At one point, shortly after describing the psychological fevers that the physical presence of a lover can create, he says that love alone prevents the 'wings of the soul' from becoming parched and dry. If, elsewhere (in the *Phaedrus*), the strength and undisciplined nature of love is depicted as the struggle of a charioteer to control two horses, one representing physical desire and uncontrollable passion, the other a more intellectual and compassionate kind of love, here Socrates has left the chariot to ride bareback!

Pillow talk

Diotima's lesson to Socrates is that although even a wise philosopher may 'fall in love with the beauty of one particular body', they will then discover that the quality of beauty that attracted them in the first place to one lover, is in fact the same thing that attracts them to another: that the beauty of their lovers is only part of some greater 'eternal' beauty. In fact, the wisest lovers realise that the beauty of moral bodies is as nothing compared with the beauties of the mind and soul, 'so that wherever they meet with spiritual loveliness, even in the husk of an unlovely body, they will find it beautiful enough to fall in love with...'

That is good news for unlovely people, but it does not stop there. For there is beauty to be found in laws, institutions and human artefacts too, and thus 'by scanning beauty's wide horizon', the philosopher is saved from'a slavish and illiberal devotion to the individual loveliness' of a single lover. Turning their eyes towards 'the open sea of beauty' the philosophers find instead 'a golden harvest of philosophy' centered around... the knowledge of the good.

5

Follow Aristotle to find true love

Aristotle's simple philosophy is: love thyself

In an essay entitled 'The nature of true self-love' the great philosopher speaks frankly:

> Should a man love himself most, or someone else? People criticise those who love themselves most, and call them self-lovers, using this as an epithet of disgrace, and say that a bad man seems to do everything for his own sake, and the more so the more wicked he is. And so men reproach him, for instance, with doing nothing of his own accord, while the good man acts for honour's sake, and the more he does so the better he is, and will act for his friend's sake, and sacrifice his own interest.
>
> Yet the facts clash with these arguments, which is not surprising. For men say that one ought to love best one's best friend, and someone's best friend is someone who wishes well to the object of his wish for his sake, even if no one is to know of it. These attributes are found most of all in a man's attitude towards himself, and it is the same for are all the other attributes by which a friend is defined for, as we have said, it is from this relation that all the characteristics of friendship have extended to our neighbours. All the proverbs, too, agree

with this, e.g. 'a single soul', and 'what friends have is common property', and 'friendship is equality', and 'charity begins at home'; for all these marks will be found most in a man's relation to himself; he is his own best friend and therefore ought to love himself best.

Self-love is, in fact, the highest form of Aristotelian love. We must not mock the egotist of Athens: his theory is that without such a basis, no one can extend sympathy and affection to others. The self-love he recommends is not hedonistic or pleasure-driven, nor even glory-seeking, depending on the adulation of the crowd, it is instead an aspect of the pursuit of the noble and virtuous, the search for which (well, most of) the philosophers agreed must culminate in the quiet reflection of the sage. Aristotle's argument is not intended to be novel but merely to connect the dots in an existing Athenian debate. Self-love enables a man 'to contemplate worthy actions... to live pleasantly... sharing in discussion and thought'. It is 'logical love'.

Not here the sexual 'bovine' frenzy, nor even the transcendence claimed by others (notably the Indian mystics that influenced Plato) for sexual union. Because both of these depend on physical attraction, which is transitory, and Plato had already said that nothing really important is transitory. Even Aristotle's second-favourite love, the kind that leads to pleasure from social activity, particularly on behalf of the community, but also from socialising with friends, must yield way. Aristotle argues: 'One cannot be a friend to many people in the sense of having friendship of the perfect type with them, just as one cannot be in love with many people at once for love is a sort of excess of feeling, and it is the nature of such only to be felt towards one person.'

Well, yes... but a frenzy of love for yourself?

Pillow talk

While we're on the subject of excesses and bovine frenzies, Aristotle explains that 'the friendship of young people seems to aim at pleasure', because, as he puts it rather nicely, 'they live under the guidance of emotion, and pursue above all what is pleasant to themselves and what is immediately before them'. Naturally, their tastes keep changing, and their friends too. Their 'amorous' relationships depend on emotion and aim solely at pleasure: 'this is why they fall in love and quickly fall out of love, changing often within a single day'.

In a passage addressed more generally, Aristotle makes a point many 'ditched' lovers might recognise.

> Those who love for the sake of utility, love for the sake of what is useful for themselves, and those who love for the sake of pleasure do so for the sake of what is pleasant to themselves, and in neither case is the other man loved except in so far as he is useful or gives pleasure. And thus these friendships are only incidental; it is not for themselves that the other is loved, but only for what they can offer in providing some good or pleasure. Such friendships, then, are easily dissolved, if the one party is no longer pleasant or useful, the other ceases to love him.

As the contemporary American scholar, Carolyn Ray argues, for Aristotle his perfect lover will be a man (Aristotle, like all the Greek philosophers is only interested in love between men) who:

• seeks the good for the benefits it will bring Aristotle

• wants to live for Aristotle's sake

• wants to be able to spend time with Aristotle

• likes the same things and makes the same choices as Aristotle

• and shares both Aristotle's pain and his pleasures

Forget 'opposites attract'. For Aristotle, it is only a small and impeccably logical step to deduce that his true love must be Aristotle himself.

6

Locke: Marriage is a legal mechanism useful for bringing up children

It is not a form of slavery

Tall and thin with a long nose and big sad eyes like a horse, John Locke, the English philosopher who accidentally inspired two revolutions, never married or had children. Perhaps his own theory about the marriage 'contract' put him off. This is set out in his celebrated *Two Treatises on Civil Government,* alongside all sorts of talk about natural rights that are generally counted as inspiring the French and American revolutionaries.

Section 78, part of a discussion of 'Political or Civil Society', states neatly and plainly:

> Conjugal society is made by a voluntary compact between man and woman; and tho' it consist chiefly in such a communion and right in one another's bodies as is necessary to its chief end, procreation; yet it draws with it mutual support and assistance, and a communion of interests too, as necessary not only to unite their care and affection, but also necessary to their common off-spring, who have a right to be nourished, and maintained by them, till they are able to provide for themselves.

And it goes on:

Section. 79. For the end of conjunction, between male and female, being not barely procreation, but the continuation of the species; this conjunction betwixt male and female ought to last, even after procreation, so long as is necessary to the nourishment and support of the young ones… This rule, which the infinite wise maker hath set to the works of his hands, we find the inferior creatures steadily obey. In those viviparous animals which feed on grass, the conjunction between male and female lasts no longer than the very act of copulation; because the teat of the dam being sufficient to nourish the young, till it be able to feed on grass, the male only begets, but concerns not himself for the female or young, to whose sustenance he can contribute nothing.

But in beasts of prey the conjunction lasts longer: because the dam not being able well to subsist herself, and nourish her numerous off-spring by her own prey alone, a more laborious, as well as more dangerous way of living, than by feeding on grass, the assistance of the male is necessary to the maintenance of their common family, which cannot subsist till they are able to prey for themselves, but by the joint care of male and female. The same is to be observed in all birds, (except some domestic ones, where plenty of food excuses the cock from feeding, and taking care of the young brood) whose young needing food in the nest, the cock and hen continue mates, till the young are able to use their wing, and provide for themselves.

Locke's bureaucratic vision of marriage includes concepts such as 'care and affection' and 'mutual support', but these are not so much romantic as legalistic. Properly understood, the marriage contract, consists chiefly in:

> ... the spouses' communion and right in one
> another's bodies

The aim and function is simply to continue the species, and love is merely the lubricating oil.

For Locke, the only special thing about the marriage contract, as opposed to other contracts for, say, washing laundry, or maybe selling slaves, is that it cannot be entered into by any two (or more) sane adults, but is restricted to two particular parties, one of whom must be a man and the other a woman. Furthermore, in Locke's theory, the original husband 'must have exercised conjugal right over his wife before he became a father' and in this way starts to exercise political authority.

The husband's dominance is the hidden contract behind the contract: the individual of 'individualism' is a man. No wonder Simone de Beauvoir later declared that 'marriage enslaves men and women to the demands of society'. In the introduction to her book, *The Second Sex* (1949), Sartre's partner says rather pointedly:

> Now, woman has always been man's
> dependant, if not his slave; the two sexes have
> never shared the world in equality. And even
> today woman is heavily handicapped, though
> her situation is beginning to change. Almost
> nowhere is her legal status the same as man's,
> and frequently it is much to her disadvantage.

> Even when her rights are legally recognised in
> the abstract, long-standing custom prevents
> their full expression in the mores. In the
> economic sphere men and women can almost
> be said to make up two castes; other things
> being equal, the former hold the better jobs,
> get higher wages, and have more opportunity

for success than their new competitors. In industry and politics men have a great many more positions and they monopolise the most important posts.

In addition to all this, they enjoy a traditional prestige that the education of children tends in every way to support, for the present enshrines the past—and in the past all history has been made by men... To decline to be the Other, to refuse to be a party to the deal—this would be for women to renounce all the advantages conferred upon them by their alliance with the superior caste.

So... is marriage a form of slavery after all?

Pillow talk

It might not count as 'feminism', but Locke does offer his own, early version of 'women's rights':

> But the husband and wife, though they have but one common concern, yet having different understandings, will unavoidably sometimes have different wills too; it therefore being necessary that the last determination, i.e. the rule, should be placed somewhere; it naturally falls to the man's share, as the abler and the stronger.

So 'yes' then, to be a wife is to become a kind of slave, and this even before kitchen sinks were invented. But 'no', too, for a moment later, Locke says:

> But this reaching but to the things of their common interest and property, leaves the wife in the full and free possession of what by contract is her peculiar right, and gives the husband no more power over her life than she has over his; the power of the husband being so far from that of an absolute monarch, that the wife has in many cases a liberty to separate from him, where natural right, or their contract allows it; whether that contract be made by themselves in the state of nature, or by the customs or laws of the country they live in; and the children upon such separation fall to the father or mother's lot, as such contract does determine.

This is liberalism, red in tooth and claw. Yes, husbands will still take the family's decisions, but they can no longer kill their wives. Yet progressive though some aspects of Locke's political philosophy seem, the fact remains that he himself was a key figure in the slave trade. He produces in his philosophical writings a weak justification for slavery, and more to the point, in administrative work as a civil servant in the New World and in England, creates a legal structure to facilitate this trade, that in his lifetime was just beginning. The bulk of the slaves were transported between 1700 and 1850, and the English ran at least one quarter of all the slave ships.

In case we might imagine that Locke had to separate his professional obligations and his private views, it should be noted that in fact these seemed to run together nicely for many years. In 1671 he bought shares in the Royal Africa Company (which used to brand each of its slaves with letters RAC) as well as, one year later, in the Bahamas Adventurers. Yet by the time his 'mature' writings appeared (notably the *Essay Concerning Human Understanding*), his position seemed to have changed. Here he describes slavery as 'so vile and miserable and Estate of Man' that is was 'hardly to be conceived that any Englishman, much less a Gentleman should plead for't.'

Could it have been a woman's influence? The idea is not so implausible. Because the most odd thing about Locke is how secretive he was about his relationships. A very different picture of the world-shaking political philosopher is painted by Wayne Glausser, in a fascinating book called *Locke and Blake: A Conversation Across the Eighteenth Century*. Here instead is a Romeo who wrote letters to young women that finish with the philosopher signing off with code-names such as 'Arricus' and even 'Philander', while the recipeients names are disguised by using initials, which are sometimes inverted and prefaced with 'Sir' instead of Madam. In 1654, Locke's enthusiasm for secrecy even leads to one woman writing back to complain about him using invisible ink.

Similarly, Locke seemed to be deep in some code when he sent another long-term pen-friend, called Elinor Parry, a raunchy French novel, about Cleopatra, and made numerous references to it in letters such as: 'the fire that ladies eyes kindle is of such a nature that death hath not coolness enough to extinguish it'. Because nothing ever seems to have come of this romantic tittle-tattle. Indeed poor Miss Parry became quite offended eventually at Locke's failure to 'follow through'. Perhaps it was this sort of thing that John Edwards, a contemporary of the two, had in mind when he dubbed Locke 'a hater of women'. Add to which that Locke wrote many times to a male friend in scathing terms about marriage calling it a fate comparable to death, and a burden. He doesn't say that in the Second Treatise!

Locke's most amorous affair seems to have been with one Damaris Cudworth, herself daughter of a respected philosopher, who he met when he was 49, a good philosophical age, and she was just 23, a bit old by Ancient Greek standards, but there we are. There are some forty letters from 'Philoclea' (Locke's code-name for Damaris) to 'Philander' (Locke's code-name for himself, but only a few of his replies.

The correspondence starts with shared philosophical interests but eventually moves towards an exchange of, well, coded poems:

I now no longer was my own:
Your friendship made me; from that hour
Was I not always in your power?
Friendship first warmed me with desire
And lodged in me a secret fire…

So wrote Locke. But he distinguishes also love from sexual appetite, the latter being only 'a toy/To please some idle, wanton boy'.

Wayne Glausser suggests that the relationship that Locke

really wanted was in fact more like that of a mother figure: Damaris is valued only as a source of comfort and reassurance. If Locke's plan would have extended eventually to marriage and intimacy, no one will ever know because events took their own course, in 1683 when Locke abruptly fled England to seek political sanctuary in Holland. At this point, Damaris' letters become just a little 'edgy', and she seems to tease him with talk of her too leaving England, but in her case to go to a different part of Holland to join a radical community called the Labadists. What was radical about them? They had abolished private property. Locke, the philosopher who built his entire system of state and family on the notion of private property could hardly have liked this talk. (Indeed, he visits the community and writes back firmly to warn her against them.)

Two years later Damaris married someone else, a knight of the realm and a widower who already had nine children. But there is a happy-ish end to this otherwise rather sad tale or unrequited love with the philosopher. On Locke's return to England from Holland, Damaris, now Lady Masham, invited him to lodge in their fine family home —and he accepts. Locke soon 'filled his rooms with own furniture and it was not long before his belongings had spilled over in to other parts of the house… his rooms looked out onto a lawn and garden in which he liked to sit in fine weather to read.' Theirs was truly a 'Platonic' relationship. Although, among the gifts he gave to her were… two rings, one of a ruby and one of a diamond.

7

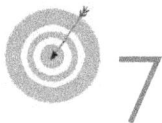

Wink at Nietzsche: Women are a dangerous play-thing

Men should seek 'the orgiastic' through destruction instead

> The true man wants two things: danger and play. For that reason he wants woman, as the most dangerous plaything.

But in what way is she dangerous? After all, elsewhere Nietzsche sums up Christianity, that despised creed, as having been invented for women, as otherwise 'One-half of mankind is weak, typically sick, changeable, inconstant… women need a religion 'that glorifies being weak, loving, and being humble as divine', or worse, make the strong weak. 'Woman has always conspired with the types of decadence, the priests, against the 'powerful', the 'strong', the men.' (As he writes in his book, *The Will to Power.*)

For today's philosophy professors, who are almost invariably men, Nietzsche is something of a hero. This is because he wrote wildly opinionated texts on religion, morality, contemporary culture, philosophy, and science, without doing anything dull like research, all the while defying conventional ethics and dazzling with savage wit, metaphor, irony, and aphorism. Hitler liked him too, even printing a special 'trench-ready' edition of the philosopher for the soldiers in the Second World War, an association that Nietzschephiles are at pains to explain away as a 'misunderstanding' of the subtly of this great thinker.

Some people say that it was his sister who distorted his views and introduced the nasty bits. But Hitler had it basically right. In his Notebook 5 for example, the unedited Nietzsche writes:

> I dream of a collective of men who are
> absolute, who know no consideration, and
> who want to be called 'destroyers'.

Pillow talk

But let's have a look for ourselves. Here is Nietzsche's most complete account of his views on 'Old and Young Women'. Which are the same, although the democratic flourish is reduced because the intention is to show all kinds of women are equally bad. Section XVIII in his book *Thus Spake Zarathustra*, starts, bluntly enough by saying that 'Everything in woman is a riddle, and everything in woman hath one solution: it is called pregnancy.' He then explains that a man is for woman always a means to an end, and the end is always a child. But what is the purpose of a woman for a man, he asks? It is here that Nietzsche offers his insight into the needs of real men:

> Two different things wanteth the true man:
> danger and diversion. Therefore wanteth he
> woman, as the most dangerous plaything.

In the modernised form, this is one of those much-quoted Nietzscheisms. It seems to offer women a rather exciting role, perhaps that of being what the French call the 'femme fatale'. But the reality is far from this:

> Man shall be trained for war, and woman for
> the recreation of the warrior: all else is folly.

If you are still tempted to read something romantic here, a few lines later we are told:

> Whom hateth woman most? Thus spake the
> iron to the loadstone: 'I hate thee most,
> because thou attractest, but art too weak to
> draw unto thee.

Two thirds of Nietzsche's writings are in the form of unpublished notes; drafts for essays and books, and that's not counting letters and correspondence. This provides a treasure trove of Nietzschean aphorisms and quotes for specialists and non-specialists alike.

The books and the notes are preoccupied with the same themes: the role and conception of tragedy in Ancient Greece; the importance of art, music and culture to society and life; the nature and task of the genius or 'higher specimens'. The notes sum up Nietzsche's metaphysics: his attitude towards knowledge, truth and goodness.

Knowledge, as sought by the scientists, merely drives us towards our 'downfall'. Truth is an obstacle, because the true philosopher makes the world through 'self-awareness'. As for goodness, 'Notebook 33' offers that 'human virtue is nothing, but human wisdom a great deal'. Such talk inspired many in the so called 'continental tradition' of philosophy: existentialism, post-modernism, and post-structuralism.

Nietzsche's short career started as a scholar of classical texts before turning to philosophy. He was appointed to the Chair of Classical Philology at the University of Basel (the youngest individual to have held this position) at the age of twenty-four, but resigned ten years later due to health problems. In 1889, now aged forty-four, he suffered a breakdown that brought to an end all philosophising.

This is the Nietzsche who sees women as the warrior's playthings, who writes of the 'Dionysian joy' of destruction, who was proud to declare his amorality, to be above the common mass. Yet Nietzsche was a lifelong bachelor—worse! He proposed to two women—both of whom rejected the offer. Nietzsche eventually went insane due to a syphilitic infection, it has long been said, as a result of sexual intercourse with a prostitute. That would be ironic, if true. But what is more substantial, as well as known for sure, is that after he became ill in 1889, at the age of forty-four, with progressive loss of his mental faculties, he lived his remaining years in the care of two women. First of all, with his mother, until her death in 1897, and then with his sister up to his own sad and rather ignominious death in 1900.

> Thou goest to women? Do not forget thy whip!

Thus spake Zarathustra.

8

Discover Heidegger's secret love

Hint: it is not a person

For the pre-war German philosopher, Martin Heidegger, love is a serious business. But not exactly in the sense hippies might hope for. Rather than wear a flower in his hair, Heidegger made a point of wearing a swastika on his jacket and rather than go to pop concerts, he liked to attend Nazi Party meetings. And rather than preach free love for the young men and women in his charge he taught them the higher love of service to the State.

But that said, there is a hippy aspect to Heidegger. Like many a later flower-child, he is concerned about what the French existentialists and other idealists called 'authenticity'. 'Being' (or 'existence') is the key concept in Heidegger's philosophy, bringing with it careful examination of all the elements that he thinks make up the fundamental aspects of human existence.

Unfortunately, Heidegger's depressing view is that these are things such as irritation, anxiety, boredom, fear and above all, death. Love and emotional attachment don't come into it. After all, as he asks his audience at the end of his inaugural lecture, *Was ist Metaphysik? (What is Metaphysics?)*, when he took over as Professor at Freiburg: 'Why are there beings at all, why not rather nothing?'

Thus, the only love that was able to inspire Heidegger was for something beyond mere human individuals. His weighty philosophy talks of 'creating the granite foundation upon which someday a state will rest that represents not a mechanism alien to our people... a *völkisch* organism: A Germanic state of the German nation'. He goes unambiguously on:

> Only where leader and led together bind each other in one destiny, and fight for the realisation of one idea, does true order grow. Then spiritual superiority and freedom respond in the form of deep dedication of all powers to the people, to the state, in the form of the most rigid training, as *commitment*, resistance, solitude, and love. The existence and the superiority of the Führer sink down into *being*, into the soul of the people and thus bind it *authentically* and passionately to the task.

And so to Heidegger's final rousing vision:

> And when the people feel this dedication, they will let themselves be led into the struggle, and they will want and sacrifice themselves. With each new moment the Führer and the people will be bound more closely in order to realise the essence of their state, that is the *Being*; growing together, they will appose the two threatening forces, death and the devil, that is impermanence and the falling away from one's own essence, with their meaningful, historical *Being* and Will.

Heidegger, perhaps we should mention, is still considered the greatest thinker of the Twentieth Century by most philosophers. They, like the post-war de-Nazification tribunal, forgive him the youthful attraction to Nazism, that caused him to join the Nazi Party, expel his Jewish colleagues and choose for himself the title of University *Führer*. Today, Hitler's political influence has faded somewhat, yet philosophy remains deeply in Heidegger's thrall.

One reason for that is the opinion of Hannah Arendt, a former student of Heidegger's, unambiguously Jewish—and rapidly becoming (hush) a philosophical figure in her own right. Arendt was solicited to write an essay for an anthology honouring the author of *Being and Time* on the occasion of his eightieth birthday. She started by recalling how she herself first heard of Heidegger, back in the Germany of the 1920s.

> There was hardly more than a name, but the name travelled all over Germany like the rumour of the hidden king. The rumour about Heidegger put it quite simply: Thinking has come to life again... There exists a teacher; one can perhaps learn to think.

Quite what he thought then, evidently was less of an issue. But she offers the following explanation of Heidegger's political activities, recalling learnedly how Plato had travelled to Syracuse to advise its tyrannical ruler, too. 'Now we all know that Heidegger, too, once succumbed to the temptation to change his *residence* and to get involved in the world of human affairs', she starts indulgently, After his relatively brief foray into politics, Plato had had to return to Athens, concluding that further attempts to put his theories into practice were futile. Heidegger though, '... was served somewhat worse than Plato because the tyrant and his victims were not located beyond the sea, but in his own country.' And she continues:

> We who wish to honour the thinkers, even if our own residence lies in the midst of the world, can hardly help finding it striking and perhaps exasperating that Plato and Heidegger, when they entered into human affairs, turned

to tyrants and Führers. This should be imputed not just to the circumstances of the times and even less to performed character, but rather to what the French call a *deformation professionelle*. For the attraction to the tyrannical can be demonstrated theoretically in many of the great thinkers (Kant is the great exception). And if this tendency is not demonstrable in what they did, that is only because very few of them were prepared to go beyond 'the faculty of wondering at the simple' and to 'accept this wondering as their abode.

In this way, Arendt, even manages to make Heidegger into the victim who fell prey to the greatness of his thought. Indeed, he emerges from the affair with some credit:

Heidegger himself corrected his own 'error' more quickly and more radically than many of those who later sat in judgement over him.

Pillow talk

Mmmm... this is complicated stuff. Let's instead look at Heidegger's own love life for insights.

On the surface, Heidegger's personal life was very conventional: he married Elfride Petri on the 21st of March, 1917, in a Catholic ceremony officiated by his friend Engelbert Krebs, who like Heidegger liked to give stirring sermons about the beauty of sacrifice for the love of the nation. Under the surface, however, things were rather more exciting. Although Martin and Elfride's first son Jörg was born promptly but respectably enough in 1919, the second child, Hermann, however, appeared to defy the laws of human biology by appearing in 1920 after a period when Heidegger had been in Italy. In fact Hermann was the love-child of Elfride and a long-standing friend of hers called Friedel Caesar. If Heidegger was put out at this dalliance, he probably had to set it alongside his taste for extramarital affairs with his students. Two such affairs are well known, one with Elisabeth Blochmann and another with... Hannah Arendt.

It is the affair with Hannah Arendt, then an 18-year-old student of the famous professor, that is the most revealing. Hannah had something of a crush on the then 35-year-old married man, which soon developed into a secret romance after Heidegger invited her to see him in his office late one evening. Subsequently, they pursued the relationship with clandestine signals such as,'If you see a light in my office at exactly 9 P.M., you can come' or alternatively in Arendt's attic room where the only witness to worry about was her little roommate, a mouse, that she fed. The affair was spiced with a sense of the danger, the need for secrecy.

Heidegger always intended it to be kept secret too, telling his 'saucy wood nymph' firmly that she must destroy all his letters after reading them. Of course, she didn't (unprincipled woman!) so years later the other 'Heidegger Affair' came to light. So the world can read salacious thoughts like this one from Heidegger to Hannah, dated the 22nd of June 1925:

> What no one ever appreciates is how experimenting with oneself and, for that matter, all compromises, techniques, moralising, escapism, and closing off one's growth can only inhibit and distort the providence of Being.

Surely no one should lightly intrude on such personal feelings. But we must! Truth demands it. So here too, is a fragment from one of Hannah's letters, four years later, after their ways had necessarily separated:

> I often hear things about you, but always with the peculiar reserve and indirectness that is simply part of speaking the famous name— that is, something I can hardly recognise. And I would indeed so like to know—almost tormentingly so—how you are doing, what you are working on, and how Freiburg is treating you.

With significance, she signs off, 'I kiss your brow and eyes', whereas Heidegger signs himself tersely, 'your'.

After the war, when many pro-Nazi academics were severely punished, the Nuremburg Tribunal (noting that Heidegger shared something of Hitler's messianic style of delivery) merely banned Heidegger from lecturing for five years. The Tribunal was influenced by the evidence on his behalf from students, Hannah Arendt, not so much because she was Jewish, but (like him) was seen as a great philosopher. Without troubling the world with trivial information on their personal relationship, Arendt painted a sufficiently generous picture of her former Professor that Heidegger was never even obliged to recant his advocacy for the Nazi project.

As to the Holocaust itself, after the war, Heidegger made only one statement: he equated it with the mechanisation of the food industry, saying that, 'in essence', food production was 'no different than the production of corpses in the gas chambers and death camps'. Both, he suggests, are examples of 'nihilism'.

9

Beware Freud: Sex is all about guilt

Add to which, birds in dreams are sexual symbols that represent the penis

---

That great philosopher, not so much of mind but of *minds*, Sigmund Freud, once described a nightmare about his mother from which he awoke in tears, screaming. The dream came during a period when Freud was making a determined effort to 'know himself' (as the Oracle at Delphi famously advised all of us to try to do). Martin Bergmann, a professor of psychology at New York University, reports how Freud carried the dream all his life, and that not only was it a nightmare at the time, but that he could never forget it.

The profoundly disturbing and horrifying dream was very vivid. At the centre of it, his 'beloved mother appears, with a peculiarly calm, sleeping facial expression', being carried into the room by people with bird beaks.

The dream led Freud to an insight, that dreams were riddles, that hid their secrets by playing with words and symbols. The subconscious mind sends the conscious mind coded messages this way. In this case, the German word *vogel*, means 'bird'. The plural of the word, *vogeln* however, is a crude German term for having sex.

When he realised this, Freud understood that the anxiety the dream caused him must have stemmed from a hidden and obscured 'sexual craving'. The root of this was a deeply suppressed wish that caused him to feel guilty: his lust for his mother violated the taboo against incest that is common to every religion and culture.

Together, the dream and Freud's analysis of it gave rise to one of his most famous ideas—the Oedipus complex—named after the Greek legend in which a man unwittingly kills his father and marries his mother. As he put it:

> I have found in my own case the phenomena of being in love with my mother and jealous of my father, and I now consider it a universal event in early childhood…

The desire of a young boy, Freud later maintained, is to replace his father as the sole recipients of his mother's affections, which can lead to an unconscious wish for his father's death. In this way, sexual attraction is framed by suppressed desires and guilt. All young children, he believed, desire having sex with their opposite-sex parent. Later, these desires become submerged and reappear as 'legitimate' sexual attraction toward adult strangers.

Pillow talk

Freud writes too that parental authority creates a more general confusion and shame in the child's mind as it struggles to develop an understandings of its own sexual nature. Our parents 'fuck us up' as the Hull poet, Phillip Larkin, memorably put it? (That's the most memorable part of his poetry though, mind you…) As an adult, this confused child becomes a 'patient' seeking therapy.

In an essay entitled 'Recollection, Repetition, and Working

Through', written in relation to his new technique of psycho-analysis Freud puts it like this (emphasis added):

> ...the patient does not say that he remembers how defiant and critical he used to be in regard to the authority of his parents, but he behaves in that way towards the physician. He does not remember how he came to a helpless and hopeless deadlock in his infantile searching after the truth of sexual matters, but he produces a mass of confused dreams and associations, complains that he never succeeds at anything, and describes it as his fate never to be able to carry anything through. *He does not remember that he was intensely ashamed of certain sexual activities, but he makes it clear that he is ashamed of the treatment to which he has submitted himself, and does his utmost to keep it a secret...*

Some critics point to a certain circularity in Freud's reasoning. And surely, if the process is as universal as Freud supposes, it can hardly qualify as a problem, much less a disorder. Could it be that guilt is just another aspect of our peculiarly complex and unfathomably human minds? After all, people feel guilty about winning, or losing, or being too rich, or too poor—or just about anything really. But psychotherapists, unlike philosophers (with one or two non-notable exceptions) charge by the hour and for some at least, such simple thoughts are not very bankable.

10

Recall Rousseau: family life requires... exotic sex

But not too exotic

Jean-Jacques Rousseau senses that much of what is most valuable in life requires love on a very personal level. For him, marriage is a romantic affair, providing the wholeness that is otherwise impossible in civilisation.

As to the two varieties of human being, where:

> ... man and woman are alike we have to do with the characteristics of the species; where they are unlike, we have to do with the characteristic of sex. Considered from these two standpoints, we find so many instances of likeness and unlikeness that it is perhaps one of the greatest of marvels how nature has contrived to make two beings so like and yet so different.

Hence, Emile, his imaginary child he devises a complete life education for, will be incomplete unless he is prepared for a full sexual life and unless his sexual partner, Sophy, is also educated in a way that will foster significant and lasting sexual commitment. Rousseau puts it this way, writing unabashedly from the male perspective:

> A woman's education must therefore be
> planned in relation to man. To be pleasing in
> his sight, to win his respect and love, to train
> him in childhood, to tend him in manhood, to
> counsel and console, to make his life pleasant
> and happy, these are the duties of woman for
> all time, and this is what she should be taught
> while she is young. The further we depart from
> this principle, the further we shall be from our
> goal, and all our precepts will fail to secure her
> happiness or our own.

Yet, despite his reputation as a scoundrel towards the fair sex, indeed his actions as a scoundrel, in some passages Rousseau displays a great sympathy for the social problems women face. Like men, they have urgent desires, but unlike men, they have far less freedom to meet those desires, and the price of making a mistake is far greater for women than for men.

> Has not a woman the same needs as a man,
> but without the same right to make them
> known? Her fate would be too cruel if she had
> no language in which to express her legitimate
> desires except the words which she dare not
> utter.

And so Sophy must be educated so that she can control Emile in subtle ways, without his realising it.

The second important principle in Rousseau's analysis of the sexes is his strong insistence that the very basis of a moral society is a nuclear family: a husband and wife charged with the responsibility of creating a home and raising children. This vision of the family brings with it the institutionalisation of sexuality, the creation of a lasting monogamous relationship fuelled by love.

Curiously though, history records that Rousseau himself had five children with an illiterate seamstress, and abandoned every child to orphanages. Rousseau's philosophy makes no attempt to match his actions, far less *vice versa*— for Rousseau to live up to his ideals.

Similarly, Rousseau's arguments, if not his actions, were also at odds with the views of other 'Enlightenment' figures of the time. *Bien pensants,* in the sense of well-intentioned thinkers, such as Voltaire and Mary Wollstonecraft, said that we ought to treat the problems of sexuality either through free love and casual liaisons, or by attacking the notion of the family unit itself. This, of course, being one of the cornerstones of Plato's analysis of the problems of society, just as it is later a key element in Marxist thought. Feminist philosophers still argue that sexual passion should not be a major priority in family relationships and often insist that the family should not be treated as the core unit of society, but rather that we should make it a great deal easier, as we have done, for women and men and children simply to opt out of family life, in the name of freedom and independence and equality.

But Rousseau specifically argues against the idea of those who (like Plato) think that a better, fairer society can only be built be dismantling the family structures first.'Will the bonds of convention hold firm without some foundation in nature? Can devotion to the state exist apart from the love of those near and dear to us? Can patriotism thrive except in the soil of that miniature fatherland, the home? Is it not the good son, the good husband, the good father, who makes the good citizen?' he asks.

Pillow talk

In his *Confessions*, Rousseau recounts in salacious detail his relationships with upper-class women such as Madam de Larange, Madame de Savoy and Madame de Warrens. As he says, 'Seamstresses, chambermaids, or milliners, never tempted me; I sighed for ladies!'

However, these were imaginary liaisons.

> I know not when I should have done, if I was to enter into a detail of all the follies that affection for my dear Madam de Warrens made me commit. When absent from her, how often have I kissed the bed on a supposition that she had slept there; the curtains and all the furniture of my chamber, on recollecting they were hers, and that her charming hands had touched them; nay, the floor itself, when I considered she had walked there. Sometimes even in her presence extravagancies escaped me, which only the most violent passions seemed capable of inspiring; in a word, there was but one essential difference to distinguish me from an absolute lover, and that particular renders my situation almost inconceivable.

It was not 'vanity of riches or rank' that attracted him, rather it was fine hands, a well-turned ankle, ribbons, lace, and well-dressed hair... altogether 'an air of delicacy and neatness throughout the whole person'. Even those with less natural beauty caught Rousseau's fancy, he says, provided always that they were 'elegantly decorated'.*

Strange then, that his first 'serious' relationship was with one Thérèsa le Vasseur, a servant in a hotel in Paris that he sometimes stayed at. She does not seem to fit the criteria at all! Writing in the mid-20th century, Bertrand Russell, who had three wives himself, says disapprovingly that no one has ever understood what attracted him to Thérèsa, adding that everyone agrees she was 'ugly and ignorant,' but perhaps here, Russell reveals more about himself than Rousseau.

When Thérèsa is introduced in the *Confessions*, it is as a girl of good family; her father an officer in the mint of Orleans, and her mother a shopkeeper. The family had fallen on hard times, and so had come to Paris where all three were supported by her selfless hard work.

Rousseau says:

> She neither knows how to count money, nor to reckon the price of anything. The word which when she speaks, presents itself to her mind, is frequently opposite to that of which she means to make use. I once made a dictionary of her phrases, to amuse M. de Luxembourg, and her *qui pro quos* often became celebrated among those with whom I was most intimate.

> But this person, so confined in her intellects, and, if the world pleases, so stupid, can give excellent advice in cases of difficulty. In Switzerland, in England, and in France, she frequently saw what I had not myself perceived; she has often given me the best advice I could possibly follow; she has rescued me from dangers into which I had blindly precipitated myself, and in the presence of princes and the great, her sentiments, good sense, answers, and conduct have acquired her universal esteem, and myself the most sincere congratulations on her merit. With persons whom we love, sentiment fortifies the mind as well as the heart; and they who are thus attached, have little need of searching for ideas

elsewhere. *I lived with my Thérèsa as agreeably
as with the finest genius in the world.*

Perhaps Russell never read the *Confessions* before
condemning Rousseau, or perhaps he simply did not recognise
what Rousseau describes there. It is a simple affection of a
kind that is not at all intellectual.

> The heart of my Thérèsa was that of an angel;
> our attachment increased with our intimacy,
> and we were more and more daily convinced
> how much we were made for each other.
> Could our pleasures be described, their
> simplicity would cause laughter. Our walks,
> *tête-à-tête,* on the outside of the city, where I
> magnificently spent eight or ten *sols* in each
> Ale house.

> Our little suppers at my window, seated
> opposite to each other upon two little chairs,
> placed upon a trunk, which filled up the space
> of the embrasure. In this situation the window
> served us as a table, we breathed the fresh air,
> enjoyed the prospect of the environs and the
> people who passed; and, although upon the
> fourth story, looked down into the street as
> we ate.

That said, Russell can call upon textual support from Rousseau
himself, who records shamelessly that he told Thérèsa that
although he would never leave her, he would not marry her
either; that her mother and her family used him simply as a
source of easy money; and finally that she was not even
faithful to him, running after 'stable boys', particularly in later
life. Scarcely, it would seem, the appropriate relationship for
the founder of Romanticism. Of some relevance here is the
story told that when James Boswell volunteered to bring
Rousseau his mistress over from France to join David Hume
in England, *en route* he took the opportunity to seduce

Thérèse—not once but thirteen times—before arriving at their destination.

> Yesterday morning had gone to bed very early,
> and had done it once: thirteen in all. Was
> really affectionate to her.

Or so the celebrated diarist wrote in his journal. This reflects poorly upon Boswell *qua* English gentleman and perhaps contributes to Rousseau's suspicions about Hume's help, but at least Boswell was suitably admonished afterwards by Thérèse. She told him that his lovemaking was vigorous but unsophisticated—although the put-down was softened as she then offered to give him lessons.

Perhaps surprisingly, Rousseau did eventually do 'the decent thing' and marry his mistress. Strictly speaking the marriage was illegal, as she was a Protestant and he was a Catholic (sort of). And the marriage lasted until death split the two apart again.

Rousseau's personal life is like his philosophy: a grand construction, implausible, unrealistic maybe, and full of unforeseen and often unfortunate consequences. Yet perhaps in the limited case of personal relationships, his failings also serve as evidence for his theory. At least Rousseau, rare amongst the philosophers, seems eventually to have discovered some genuine feeling for his life-long partner.

---

* As ever, there is a gap between Rousseau's theory and the practice. One promisingly steamy encounter with a beautiful, Italian women called Zulietta founders in the bedroom because Rousseau is put off by a malformity of one of her nipples, a failure of ardour on his part that he bitterly reproaches himself for later. Wqually bitterly, she advises him to 'leave women and study mathematics'.

Cast of Philosophical Characters

Saint Thomas Anselm (1033–1109)

Anselm was an eleventh century Italian Benedictine monk, who became Archbishop of Canterbury in England. He was a philosopher–theologian, credited with the first 'ontological' (from the Latin for the study of 'being') theory of the existence of God. This stated that God, being the greatest possible object of thought, cannot lack existence–otherwise He would not be the greatest.

Aristotle (384–322 BCE)

Aristotle (like all the other Ancient philosophers) made no distinction between scientific and philosophical investigations. He was particularly interested in observing nature and his biology was much admired by Darwin amongst others. Aristotle influenced subsequent studies by his view that organisms had a function, were striving towards some purposeful end, and that nature is not haphazard. If plant shoots are observed to bend towards the light they are 'seeking the light'. The function of mankind is, he suggests, to reason, as this is what people are better at than any other member of the animal kingdom - 'Man is a rational animal'. This approach is in contrast to that of today's biologist or scientist who try to explain things by reference to 'mechanisms'. (As if they explain anything!)

Simone de Beauvoir (Capricorn, January 9, 1908–86)

The conventional view of Simone de Beauvoir is that she is a minor figure, forever in the shadow of her lifelong intellectual confidant and companion Jean Paul Sartre. Some people, however, would make her the true founder of the movement known as existentialism. At least her book, The Second Sex (1949), is now accepted as a key text in modern feminist thinking.

Jeremy Bentham (Aquarius, February 15 1748–1832)

Bentham was descended from two generations of lawyers and his approach is legalistic, although he himself decided that the more useful question was how the law ought to be rather than what it actually was. He argues too that what his contemporaries were celebrating as 'natural rights' were little more than imaginary rights, and actual law created the only 'actual rights'. The French Declaration of the Rights of Man he described as 'nonsense on stilts' warning that to want something is not to supply it, that hunger is the same thing as bread. Bentham saw the world as torn between two great forces, the quest for pleasure, and the avoidance of pain and that it would be better to maximise the former and minimise the latter,

Boethius (c. 480–525 AD)

Anucius Manlius Severinus Boethius was born in Rome, studied the 'liberal arts' including philosophy and rose to become a consul, an honorary and actually rather expensive position. Boethius was part of the Roman 'establishment', entitled to be addressed as 'Your Magnitude' and was employed by the Gothic ruler, Theodoric, in various cultural pursuits such as designing a sundial and water clock for the King of Burgundy. Unfortunately, after dabbling in politically unwise areas, probably with the intention of overthrowing Theodoric for a more cultured fellow, he incurred Theodoric's displeasure, and was arrested. tried on charges of conspiracy, imprisoned in Pavia, and last but not least, executed. Stuff happens!

Chuang Tzu (369–286 BCE)

One of the great sages of Chinese philosophy, Chuang Tzu, stresses the unity of all things, and dynamic interplay of opposites. 'Good' and 'bad', he points out, are like everything else, inter-related and interchangeable. What is 'good' for the rabbit is 'bad' indeed for the farmer, to offer a rather weak example of my own. His book, the Chuang Tzu, of which about a quarter is considered to be directly attributable to 'Master Chuang' is lively and playful, a mixture of stories and poetry as well as philosophical arguments.

Confucius (551–479 BCE)

Confucius was the essence of the ancient Chinese sage, a social philosopher, an educator, and the founder of the Ru School of Chinese thought. It is said that altogether he had 3,000 disciples of whom... er, 72 were influential. Confucius presents himself as a transmitter who invented nothing and his greatest emphasis may be the one on learning from the ancient sages. In this respect, he is mostly respected by Chinese people as a Great Teacher or Master. According to Confucius, musical training is the most effective method for changing the moral character of man and keeping society in order.

René Descartes (Aries, March 31, 1596–1650)

Mathematician, scientist, and philosopher, born March 31, 1596 in La Haye, France. Descartes was educated at a highly religious Jesuit college, but joined the army in 1618 in order, as he put it, to travel widely for the next 10 years. In 1628 he settled in Holland, where he would remain for most of his life. Descartes' aim was to bring to philosophy the rigour and clarity of mathematics. His most influential book, *Meditations on First Philosophy* (1641), introduces what has become known as the 'method of doubt, the use of which requires all and any things about which it is possible 'to be deceived' to be rejected. Knowledge based on sense perception, that from books or other authorities must be set aside, but so also must knowledge involving reasoning that is inadequately founded on certain 'indubitable' truths - all in order to arrive at something about which we can be absolutely certain. This point, it turns out, is summed up in the famous Latin phrase, *cogito ergo sum* , usually translated as 'I think therefore I am', although that is, in itself anything but uncontroversial. By splitting the universe into two forever opposed parts, mind and matter, he created insoluble problems for understanding consciousness, motivations, and the world around us.

Diogenes of Sinope (c. 400–325 BC)

Born in Sinope on the southern shore of the Black Sea, Diogenes 'the Cynic' later moved to Athens and may have spent some time in Corinth. He is renowned for his controversial behaviour, recorded in Book Six of Diogenes Laertius. His austere and uncompromising way of life led Plato to call him a 'Socrates gone mad'.

Epictetus (CE 55–135)

Epictetus was born a slave in present-day Turkey), and 'worked' (so to speak) in Rome until his banishment, when he went to Greece for the rest of his life. His teachings were written down and published by his pupil Arrian in his *Discourses*. Epictetus' advice is great for self-help gurus. He advises us that 'external' events are caused by fate, and are thus beyond our control, and thus that we should accept whatever happens calmly and dispassionately. Unhappiness and suffering are caused not by events, but by trying to control what is outside our power. We are only responsible for own actions, which we should always think carefully about and control through rigorous self-discipline.

Sigmund Freud (Taurus 6 March 1856–1939, but 'officially'' Pisces, May 6)

Freud was born in nineteenth century Moravia, then part of the Austro-Hungarian empire, to a secular, middle class Jewish family. His views of how the mind really works have influenced our view of ourselves. Freud argues that human beings are driven by *libido*, a powerful sexual impulse. He observed in his patients that *libido* could be directed towards many objects, which sometimes led to internal conflict. The attempt to repress what were felt to be forbidden desires could produce symptoms.

G.W.F Hegel, (Virgo, August 27 1770–1831)

Georg Wilhelm Friedrich Hegel was born in Stuttgart and educated at Tübingen seminary, alongside the epic poet Friedrich Hölderlin and fellow philosopher Friedrich Schelling. With the exception of a brief period as a newspaper editor, Hegel devoted his life wholly to teaching, first at Jena, then Nuremberg, Heidelberg, and finally Berlin. The first two posts were in schools, only the latter ones from 1816, where as a university 'professor'. Some consider Hegel's thought to represent the summit of 19th Century Germany's movement of philosophical idealism; it led to the 'historical materialism' of Karl Marx, but also, as is less often noted, to the development of the fascist ideology in Italy, Spain and Germany. The ideologies are all united in a view of the individual as merely a cog in the state machine.

Martin Heidegger, (Libra, September 26 1889–1976)

Jean-Paul Sartre may be 'the father of existentialism' for the general public, but it is Martin Heidegger who holds this proud title amongst the European philosophers. Naturally, he rejected 'existentialism' as a gross oversimplification, admitting only to the rather airy study of 'being'. Being and Time (*Sein und Zeit*) paved the way in 1927, following on several journal articles broadly concerned with rejecting the 'idealism' of Kant for a more modern 'critical realism'. It is here that Heidegger explains that the problem for humanity, with its conscious awareness of its existence (Dasein as he puts it), 'lies in its always having its being to be'.

David Hume (Taurus, April 26 1711–76)

Hume was born into a devoutly observant Scottish Presbyterian family, and initially was intended to take up law. But from the age of 17 he instead began work on a great philosophical project that would in due course, wake the philosophical world from its dogmatic slumber, as Kant aptly put it, recording his own debt to Hume.

Immanuel Kant (Aries, April 22 1724–1804)

Kant's philosophical career reflects the breadth of his teaching and his interests. When, after 1770, he finally came to write the works for which he is most famous, namely the three Critiques, he addressed what he saw as the fundamental questions that cover human concerns: 'what can I know?', 'what ought I do?' and 'what may I hope for?'

Lao Tzu (c. sixth century BCE)

Lao Tzu is revered in China as one of the three great sages, but barely acknowledged in the West. The story goes that one day

Lao Tzu was unhappy with China and wanted to leave it to travel, but a the frontier a guard recognised him as the great sage and refused to let him pass unless he first recorded all his wisdom on parchment. Because of, or perhaps despite, being indubitably very wise, Lao Tzu managed to do this in just a few weeks, producing a volume of a little over 5000 Chinese characters.

Gottfried Leibniz (Cancer, July 1 1646–1716)

Leibniz was born in Berlin and later became on the founders of its academy. 'An elegant man in a powdered wig', as one contemporary summed him up, Leibniz spent most of his life deep in philosophic contemplation, revealing himself to the world only through learned correspondences with several hundreds of other philosophers and scientists. Nonetheless, his influence in seventeenth century intellectual circles was great, much to the envy of Sir Isaac Newton, his rival for the honour of being first to invent calculus.

John Locke (Virgo, August 29 1632-1704)

John Locke was born in a quiet Somerset village into a Puritan trading family, and into a rather less quiet period of Civil War between Parliament and Royalists. He argues that people all have certain fundamental 'rights' and also attempts to return the other half of the human race, the female part, to their proper, equal, place in history, the family and in government. His writings are the first, essentially practical, even legalistic, framework and analysis of the workings of society.

John Stuart Mill (Taurus, May 20 1806–1873)

Mill was born in London, son of James Mill, and worked at the East India Company with a brief spell as a Member of Parliament, particularly interested in women's rights, constitutional reform and economics. He met Harriet Taylor , of whom he says in his *Autobiography*, that he owes none of his 'technical doctrines' but all of the liberal ideas. Mill says that allowing people to decide for themselves as much as possible increases the general happiness, arguing in favour of liberty of thought, speech and association.

Friedrich Nietzsche (Libra, October 15 1844–1900)

Nietzsche was born in the Prussian town of Röcken during a period of political and economic ferment. His central interests were the 'death of God' and with it, he claimed, the 'slave morality' of Christianity with its elevation of self-sacrifice and pity over what he considered the true virtue: the pursuit of power. For Nietzsche, all human beings, and indeed all life, are engaged in this struggle to increase their power. Declaring himself to be the 'first immoralist', he promised to 'revalue' all values, starting with the unmasking of Christianity and literally making 'good', 'bad'. He was unable to complete this task as, in 1889, he descended into a twilight of his own, never emerging from madness.

Plato (427-347 BCE)

Plato was born, studied, taught, and died in Athens, albeit with some travelling in-between. His dialogues, apparently recording historical conversations between Socrates and various fellow citizens of the city, range widely, from the distinction between mind and matter, echoed later by Descartes and to the strange theory of heavenly ideas, or forms, one of which exists for every concept we have. However, it is clear from his elevation of the 'Form of the Good', and his metaphor of the Cave, (both in the Republic) that ethics is the central concern to which he always returns. The shackled prisoners can only be 'set free' when they let the light thrown out by knowledge of the good illuminate their miserable earthbound existence.

Plutarch (CE 46–119)

Plutarch was a biographer and author of perhaps 227 works, the best known of which is *Parallel Lives*. In this he recounts the noble deeds and characters of Greek and Roman soldiers, legislators, orators, and statesmen. His next-best effort is *Moralia*, or *Ethica*, a series of more than 60 essays on ethical, religious, physical, political, and literary topics.

Pythagoras (born c. 570 BCE)

Pythagoras was born on the island of Samos. He not only made important contributions to music and astronomy, metaphysics, natural philosophy, politics and theology, he was the first person to bring the concepts of reincarnation, heaven and hell to the Western world, declaring that the doctrines were a personal revelation to himself from God. Pythagoras is often misrepresented. A recent description has him part priest, part philosopher, part conjurer, who wore a white robe, trousers and a coronet and appealed to the authority of poetry. All of this can be derived from the ancient literature but is misleading. Perhaps it is because of the strict rules governing study at his school, particularly about what to eat - his vegetarianism.

Jean Jacques Rousseau (Cancer, June 28 1712–1778)

Rousseau was born in Geneva, and educated at home by his father, Isaac, a watchmaker, and his aunt, after the untimely death of his mother following his birth. Unfortunately, he soon lost his father too, after the latter unwisely challenged a gentleman to a duel, and was expelled from the city as a result. Jean-Jacques went into the care of his uncle, to become an apprentice engraver. But Rousseau considered this to be a demeaning trade and, using a tactic his city had demonstrated some years before to gain its independence, changed his religion to became the ward of some benevolent Catholic aristocrats. It was in their library of the great political philosophers that he imbibed the ideas of Hobbes, Machiavelli and Locke that would later inspire his influential, even revolutionary works.

In his most polemical essay, the *Discourse on Inequality* (1753) he ridicules the pretensions of 'civilisation' , nor is he impressed by the achievements of science. Instead he argues that primitive peoples had been happier and better off.

Jean Paul Sartre (Cancer, June 21 1905–1980)

Sartre's philosophy emphasises the use of the imagination, which is the purest form of freedom available to us. In his *Critique of Dialectical Reason* he offers by way of an example, workers engaged in monotonous tasks who he says are prone to having sexual fantasies, thus demonstrating the power and counter-factual freedom of the imagination. This spotlight on 'consciousness' is what made Sartre's name. Curiously enough, another book that came out in 1943, She Came to Stay, by his lifelong intellectual confidant and companion, Simone de Beauvoir, also describes various kinds of consciousness. Curiouser still, Sartre records in his diary how de Beauvoir had to correct him several times for his clumsy misunderstanding of the 'existentialist' philosophy!

Arthur Schopenhauer (Pisces, February 22, 1788-1860)

Schopenhauer was born in Danzig and worked all his life in Germany, building upon and adapting Kant's philosophy with elements from Buddhism and Platonism too. Unlike his contemporaries, he quite admired much the English, noting approvingly, for example, their concern for animals. He writes, as Russell complains, of the need to penetrate the 'veil of Maya' in order to see the common reality of 'will', which is Maharakya or 'Great World', Hindu wisdom, and from Buddhism too comes his solution: nothingness. Nothingness is exactly the best you can obtain. It is the literal meaning of 'nirvana'.

Adam Smith (Gemini, June 5 1723–1790)

The first edition of An Inquiry into the Nature and Causes of the Wealth of Nations, cost one pound and sixteen shillings, and sold out within six months. Smith 's publisher, William Stahern, had just produced another best-seller: Gibbon's Decline and Fall of the Roman Empire. It was thought that Wealth of Nations was to technical for a popular readership, but Gibbon himself realised that there was a great strength to be found in Smith's book. It was there in "the most profound ideas expressed in the most perspicuous language". And it was there because the Wealth of Nations is, despite the title, not merely concerned with economics. It is a much more comprehensive vision of society, and in its pages economics is merely a by-product, albeit a necessary one, of social life. So Smith is concerned not only with money, but with justice and equity. If his findings are nowadays adopted by those of a different disposition, that is not his fault.

Socrates (470-399 BCE)

Socrates taught and discussed philosophy in Athens during the golden age of Greek philosophy, but wrote nothing himself (as far as we know). His views are relayed instead by Aristophanes in his play The Clouds, by Xenophon, in his writings, and most of all, by his pupil, Plato, in his famous dialogues or playlets. In these, Socrates is always the star, employing the characteristic method of dialectical questioning that takes his name to elicit knowledge. Nonetheless, no one can be sure that it really is Socrates who is represented there— or Plato—or even just a philosophical position. Socrates remains an enigma.

Ludwig Wittgenstein (Aries, April 26 1889-1951)

Ludwig Wittgenstein was the peculiar maths teacher-soldier-engineer, and, eventually-reluctantly-philosopher. His reputation rests on just two philosophy books. The first, in 1922, in which he numbered each sentence as he went along, in a self-conscious attempt at indicating the importance of his insights, is the *Tractatus Logico-Philosophicus*. This says that all philosophy problems have been solved. Wittgenstein was at this time distinctly logical positivist in flavour, and criticises philosophers for being vague: indeed he says, not once but twice, in the *Tractatus*: 'whereof one cannot speak, one must remain silent.' However, in his later, posthumously published book, *Philosophical Investigations*, he reversed many of his earlier findings, and compared words and sentences to the tools in a tool box, or to the controls of a locomotive, saying that meaning is use.

Zeno of Elea (fifth century BCE)

Zeno slightly predates Plato although he may have just known Socrates. He is even older than Euclid, whose fabulous geometrical systems, developed form those of the North Africans, so impressed the philosophers. But nonetheless, much of Zeno is about geometry and the nature of numbers - particularly the strange quantities infinity, and zero. He is best remembered for his four paradoxes of motion—such as the story of the race between Achilles and a Tortoise, in which it seems 'logically speaking, that the famous runner can never make up the tortoise's lead.

Further reading *Key sources and brief notes*

MAKE LOVE LIKE A PHILOSOPHER

Kant's views are set out in his lecture splendidly entitled 'On Duties to the Body in Regard to the Sexual Impulse'. The Aristotle quotations are lightly adapted from the *Nicomachean Ethics*, particularly Book VIII. Carolyn Ray presents here argument in a paper, 'Egoism in Aristotle's Nicomachean Ethics' available online at:
http://enlightenment.supersaturated.com/essays/text/carolynray/aristotle egoism.html

The discussion of 'Kant on being faithful' draws on my earlier book *Philosophical Tales* (Wiley-Blackwell 2008)

The quotes from Epictetus are adapted from the versions in *Cynics (Ancient Philosophies)*, by William Desmond, University of California Press (2008) The quotation on family values is section 3.22.77 of the *Discourses*.

The strange story of Descartes' daughter, Francine, (Tactic 41) is described in more detail in *Descartes: An Intellectual Biography*, by Stephen Gaukroger, (Oxford UP 1997) and also in an essay online at http://checkyourfacts.wordpress.com/2010/10/19/the-life-and-death-and-then-life-and-then-death-of-francine-descartes/.

There are several versions of the particular episode concerning Descartes and Francine (the automaton) on the boat - and it seems likely that none of them are true. As Stephen Gaukroger points out, Descartes was a controversial figure for years after his death, his books were on the Pope's 'banned list', and he was even accused of having created the first 'real' Francine as part of a cold, philosophical experiment into human biology.

The introduction to Simone de Beauvoir's book, *The Second Sex* (1949) explains her view that: 'woman has always been man's dependant, if not his slave'. The text can be found 'freely available' too at: http://www.marxists.org/reference/subject/ethics/de-beauvoir/2nd-sex/introduction.htm

Locke describes 'women's rights' in section 82 of *his Second Treatise of Civil Government* (1690). As to marriage being a form of slavery, it should be noted that the French philosopher, Michel de Montaigne, also describes the institution as a kind of cage, albeit (curiously) he adds that even as the birds inside try to escape, others outside are trying to get in.

Freud says that dreams are fulfilments of wishes in *The Interpretations of Dreams* (New York: Avon, 1966), 185. A contrary view appears in a collection of original papers by 'an international group of distinguished philosophers of science': *Freud and the History of Psychoanalysis*, Edited by Toby Gelfand, John Kerr (published 1992 by Routledge). If you are beginning to think that philosophers have rather a spotty line on human relationships (*vide* Andrew Schaffer and his witty and insightful little book, *Great Philosophers who Failed in* Love (Harper Collins, 2011), well, let's just say they've got a lot of explaining to do.

By the same author

If you enjoyed this, you might enjoy...

101 Philosophy Problems

Cohen continually delights or infuriates us with his irreverent
opinions. He tells us, for example, that Kant reduced philosophy 'to
esoteric monologues of professionals' and that Aristotle 'suffered
from a particularly severe taxonomical disorder'. Logic is irrelevant, a
point he reinforces by not using it to clarify philosophical problems.
    —*Times Higher Education* (London)

Are all moral claims synthetic? Or analytic? Or *a priori?* Or *a
posteriori?* Or both? Or neither? What about tables? Can you see
one? Ask yourself: does it exist? Too easy? Go out of the room and
ask yourself again. The next sentence is true. The previous sentence
is false. Obey the brain warning at the beginning and don't read all
101 problems at once. On free will: You don't always act yourself if
you're suffering from a paranoid personality disorder.
    —*The Guardian*

Without technical terms and incomprehensible superstructure, but
with wit and irony, Cohen explains the basic concepts of philosophy
and, in passing, the most famous thinkers of history.
    —*Der Spiegel*

101 Ethical Dilemmas

...a chatty, jokey journey through philosophical dilemmas, ancient and modern... but the philosophy is the real thing.
　　—*New Scientist*

There are a lot of DIY philosophy texts around—not so much takin' it to the streets as takin' it to the dinner parties... The logical positivists might have called ethics gobbledegook, but it is well and truly on the menu here in 101 courses.
　　—*The Age* (Melbourne)

Wittgenstein's Beetle

One of the fun things about philosophy as opposed to, say, chemistry is that to find things out you don't need to mess around with test tubes and Liebig condensers. Instead, you can sit back in your armchair, set up a laboratory in your own head and calmly observe the results of mixing x with y. This is the grand tradition of the 'thought experiment', to which Cohen provides a zippy alphabetical guide.
　　—*The Guardian*

With its sense of history, *Wittgenstein's Beetle* provides the opportunity to consider which thought experiments last. Some are as surprising today as when they were first mooted. Plutarch rehearsed the one about falling under gravity to the centre of the earth, and then out again the other side: it produces the amazing result that the time taken to tumble between any two cities... via the straightest tunnel connecting them... would always be forty-three minutes.
　　—*Times Literary Supplement*

The Doomsday Machine

... a polemic on the evils of splitting the atom.
—Matthew Wald, *New York Times* Green Blog

It should be compulsory reading for the many politicians who still seem to be seduced by the nuclear dream
—Paul Brown, *Climate News Network*

Philosophical Tales

In *Philosophical Tales*, Cohen presents what he calls an alternative history of philosophy that tells its story by interweaving brief biographies of the major philosophical players with brief discussions of their ideas, including many of their more frequently overlooked ideas. He attempts to show through a combination of humor and ironic irreverence that philosophy, or at least the lives of the great philosophers, is as filled with prejudices, jealousies, vanities, and ridiculous ideas, as it is with the pursuit of wisdom.

Through this unflattering tale of philosophy, Cohen aims to show that philosophers are ordinary people and that ordinary people are and should be philosophers. It is easy to suppose that Cohen's purpose is to cut to size or debunk the claims to intellectual superiority of great philosophers... Yet, if this is Cohen's purpose, it is not his only purpose. One of his important concerns is to raise some uncomfortable questions about philosophy and its great figures—questions to which historians of philosophy have not paid sufficient attention to.
—*Teaching Philosophy*

www.ingramcontent.com/pod-product-compliance
Lightning Source LLC
Chambersburg PA
CBHW020515030426
42337CB00011B/395